The Blue Cat Walks the Earth

The Blue Cat Walks the Earth
Poems by F..D. Reeve

Published 2008 by
Smokestack Books
PO Box 408, Middlesbrough TS5 6WA
e-mail : info@smokestack-books.co.uk
www.smokestack-books.co.uk

The Blue Cat Walks the Earth
F.D. Reeve
Copyright 2008 and 2009 F.D. Reeve, all rights reserved
First published by Azul Editions, USA, 2007

Printed by
EPW Print & Design Ltd

ISBN 978-0-9560341-0-6
Smokestack Books gratefully
acknowledges the support of
Middlesbrough Borough Council
and Arts Council North East

Smokestack Books is
represented by Inpress Ltd
www.inpressbooks.co.uk

Contents

7 The Illusionist
9 The Cat & the Fool
10 The Cat's Philosophy, or Having Your Cake & Eating It, Too
11 The Apology
12 Envy: Imagining the Life of a Bird
13 The Cat Declines the Temptations of Public Office
14 He Falls in Love
15 The Cat Walks Back & Forth in a Store Window
16 He Writes to His Cousin in Baghdad
17 Max Ernst's Loplop Meets Blue
19 He Honours a Friend Who Loved Music
21 The Bar & The Mirror at the Folies Bergères
23 The Blue Cat Takes Over from Miss Lonelyhearts
24 The Birdwatcher
25 May Day in Moscow
26 The Blue Cat Calls a Contry Dance
31 The Cat Remembers One of His Heroes
33 Fortune-telling
34 The Cat Ponders Joining a Picket Line
35 The Blue Cat Blues
37 An Invisible Man Addresses the Cat
39 The Auctioneer
41 The Cat Advances to a Higher Degree
43 The Heavenly Kingdom
45 The Cat Leads a Revival Meeting
48 The Blue Cat Hits the Ballot Box
49 A Blue Study: Fiscal Policy vs. Monetary

50 Acknowledgements

The Illusionist

The other day I came on the Blue Cat in the kitchen poring over our cheap, two-volume edition of the Oxford English Dictionary, sometimes laying the magnifying glass on the page and bending over it, sometimes parked on his haunches and trying to read through the glass as it slowly sank through his paws. He had just discovered the hundred-and-fifty-year-old theory that the material world is an illusion. This theory - Illusionism; its adherents were known as Illusionists - came to refer to using illusionary effects in art. The Cat loved it. Soon, he said, 'illusionist' labelled a producer of illusions- specifically, a conjurer, a magician, or, in a word, a cat. Hence, also, the title of a recent film about a Viennese magician who gets himself into social trouble by falling in love with a girl above his station. He who spends his life entertaining others by deception has to undeceive them about his passion. Illusion within illusion within illusion – what is the greatest illusion of all? 'Freedom,' said The Cat twitching his whiskers and grinning like a madman.

Corneille's *Illusion Cornique* carries no final irony: when at the end the magician shows the father his son as an actor disrobing, the only illusion remaining is that the figures on stage aren't actors, but of course they are. They're actors playing actors; so, soon they turn to the audience for appreciation – just as your cat turns to you to have his ears scratched and his belly tickled. This time out the Blue Cat may be a couple of years older, but he's still the actor he was. Perhaps more so, for the world is more sombre than ever and the threats both to human life and to the earth itself are even greater than when the Cat was a kitten. In fact, the only way he can get people to listen is to pretend he's not saying what he says – that he's an illusionist making an illusion of himself. Of course, he's telling the truth. Of course, you don't have to believe him. Nine times out of ten the truth is unbelievable.

The great illusion that underlies the illusions of art is that freedom is attainable.

The big difference between us and the Cat is that he believes in truth and freedom and is willing to lay down all his remaining lives for what he believes. We can't ask for more.

F.D. Reeve

The Cat & The Fool

The Holy Fool gives free advice:
    'Bad weather.
Grief-gatherers mass in the greenhouse,
    their feathers
dip and sway like tropical leaves.'
    'Who knows
what you know?' says the Cat. 'Is it make-believe?
    Madmen sting
the air with noise like a swarm of bees.'

    The Fool: 'Skulls
on the beach, fleas in wet sand;
    gold flakes
fall from the deciduous stars –
    break
then the salt hours like pearls,
    fish
in the trees stiff, fat
    like pears.'

The Cat: 'Cast the bones,
    doctor,
the sea is in uniform;
    Alma,
I fly!" The Fool: 'Train long gone.
    Nebulae
of ants muster in space,
    march
      across the whites of God's eyes.'

The Cat's Philosophy,
or Having Your Cake and Eating It, Too

Outdoors the air is blue with cold;
        the last apples are frozen.
All day the kitchen waits folded
        like napkins for dinner music,
footsteps, and the curtain of steam
        that rises on the evening life.

A sequence of small acts ensues—
        some prepared, some spontaneous—
then comes the dessert—wild, unreserved,
        the climactic understatement:
Making love is like painting a face
        on both sides of a window.

The Apology

The Café serves late breakfast, lunch, and tea.
It's open every day from ten to three.
    TODAY THE CAFÉ IS CLOSED.
    Sorry for the inconvenience

The things the museum keeps of historic note
are there for you to value by modern vote.
    TEMPORARILY CLOSED FOR REFURBISHMENT.
    Sorry for the inconvenience

There's a hole in the lane because they're digging again
to repair last year's relaid water mains.
    ROAD CLOSED. LOCAL ACCESS ONLY.
    Sorry for the inconvenience

In Baghdad girls—well-dressed, still alive—
run down the steps where mortar shells killed five.
    SCHOOL CLOSED UNTIL FURTHER NOTICE.
    Sorry for the inconvenience

The fighting raged through the night. As the sun rose
over the desert, the dead, and the half-burned town,
    it turned out all the streets were closed.
    Sorry for the inconvenience

Warm weather melts the polar ice; great storms
toss containers on the sea; fish swarm, not bees;
    farms are gone, mortgages, foreclosed.
    Sorry for the inconvenience

When The Cat sets out tomorrow I bet there'll be
a new sign floating on the sea:
    EARTH FOREVER CLOSED
    Sorry for the inconvenience

Envy: Imagining the Life of a Bird

High overhead I see
a wild hawk skate figure eights
on a pure glass sky;

then down, down he pirouettes
and peels shoulder-first through space
with a human cry.

The Cat Declines the Temptations of Public Office

Cruel how the faithful set limits to the soul:
    Why not torture the lecherous owl
    that tears the mouse apart and swallows the moth?
    Why not boil the firefly
    semaphoring its passion atop the hay?
    Why not castrate the lover ermined with old age?
Violence, like a habit, suits popular behaviour.

A small red spider jigging on a thread
    baits the horny imagination;
    in the outhouse shadows a girl's golden head
    dances under the full moon,
    abused, translucent, at dawn invisible.
    No trespassing without shame. The Cat watches
    followers in the crowd shift like flies on a window,
black bodies leaping up at the sun.

He Falls in Love

If I had been born to the wild where Náhani led
a timber wolf pack and fell in love with Tah Kloma,
who tracked her through the stars for three years, by day
looking for trap-deformed prints and a trail of fresh spoor;
       then found the silver-haired phantom of Tatlatui,
       the queen of the Stikine Plateau, pure natural hero,
       and travelled north in her heart to the Yukon taiga—
       wouldn't I be a part of the living world?
       wouldn't I walk in the shadow of a rainbow?

In the Trojan War, Achilles and Hector led
the painful fighting, brought down many Tah Klomas,
turned the Skamander blood-red day after day,
and searched for victory signs in bird flight and spoor;
       then history, like a wooden horse or a starved Kabuli,
       beat their swords into ploughs and trampled both
              divine heroes,
       leaving their bones for ravens down from the taiga—
       Nahani, love, I worship the living world
       and wait for my life in the shadow of a rainbow.

The Cat Walks Back & Forth in a Store Window

He sees the pattern hidden in the earth
who recalls the past as like a Persian carpet
worked by women's hands back and forth
across a loom forever—warp and woof—
the wool becoming camels and red flowers,
a desert on the floor, a knotted maze
of latitude and longitude in praise
of natural beauty and some girl's sacrifice.

Behind the glass that mirrors passersby
three families meet—the blood-related hands
that tied the yarns together, the scholar-gypsy
whose secret admiration for eastern art
opens the way to unknown excellence,
and the passive customers with uncertain hearts—
each day East underlies the West as sand
in a hourglass lays time down by artifice.

The stars are his rug across the midnight sky;
they are his light (the unthinkable is fire)—
they shine on him here where he celebrates his best
intentions and his imaginary gains;
somewhere behind them the facts of history rise
in a river of chaos as mad as Bartholomew Fair,
and space-time bends around our magnetic hearts
like the rugs that float us on exotic air.

He Writes to His Cousin in Baghdad

Anis al-Jalis, *sabah al khair!*
    Heavy storm clouds from the East
    brought the bad news: another ambush,
    this month a thousand dead, a girl—
    hope of the future—belly slit
    by shrapnel, one-legged, blood-covered, blind—
    does the army this morning roar in anger?
        do citizens shake their fists in fear?

Sweet long-haired cousin, your dark brown eyes
    bearing the burdens of Babylon
    watch over the space between time past
    and what becomes as every morning
    your two great rivers wash the night down
    and the sun rises red from the water.
    Here we curl up in the flag and say nothing:
        our public words make only lies.

I hear your voice in the twilight calm
    arising from the man-high reeds
    like Ishtar's magic above the river
    when kings and princes fell in love
    and old men stared and wagged their beards
    and young men undid their belts. O Anis,
    child of Shamash, king of heaven,
        may you live forever. *Maasalaama, maasalaama.*

Max Ernst's Loplop Meets Blue

In Paris when Blue had nothing to say
he dreamed of going to a posh café
       and in a grand, indignant way
    reciting Old French triolets.

The Deux Maggots, the Cat had heard,
        was the *echt* place to catch The Word
        where deconstruction's finger stirred
   the coffee – when behold! The Bird

Superior rose from the water glass.
      A page from the past had come to pass
      as to return to homeland grass
Joe led Mary on an ass

from Nazareth to Bethlehem.
     Can't say that trio will act again,
     but Luke portrayed them on stage then,
   and what shaped history still shapes men.

The Bird was like the moving hand
      that writ on the wall, or the Speckled Band,
      or the Sphinx astride the shifting sand—
four febrile fingers in a foreign land

of paint and symbol daring the blind
     to cross the deserts in their minds.
     Of course before comes from behind--
the world, i' faith, is a solid line

'twixt sleep and wake, a path in dream
      through silver woods, a swim upstream
     to the Cumaean spring, a beam
of light like diamonds in the seams

of gravity as black as coal
        where dead stars lie in their dead holes.
      The storied fools are Old King Cole
   (royalty exit before the toll)

and the artist who painted *La Femme 100 Têtes*
   (Wall Street crashed; the art's here yet)
    who said to The Bird, *'Loplop, grande bête,*
marotte derrière ma cuvette de toilette,

string my name across the sky
      in letters dripping gentian dye,
     then fold the future in a pie
of one-eyed jacks and blue cat's eyes.'

To The Cat The Bird bowed low to say,
    'Your natural whiskers have won the day,'
    and called to the waiter, *'Deux cafés, s'il vous plaît.'*
The sun arose in a New World way.

To dig the moral is no trick—
    cats and birds, of course, don't mix—
    and though cats may not get first pick
   they always have the final lick.

He Honours a Friend Who Loved Music

in memory of Junius Irving Scales (1920-2002)

Some people never tire
        of saying 'Where there's smoke there's fire,'
or: 'Better safe than sorry'
        and take a brolly on a night that's starry;
they think Red Reynard a clever bastard,
        quick-witted sober or half plastered;
so here's a little tale to show
        that though he's smarter than a crow
no way can he outfox The Cat.

Each time a hungry rabbit protest
        against fox monopoly of lettuce
sets off from Times Square to the Village
        or tries to stop the vulpine pillage
of druid stones and family dens,
        who lines the avenues with pens?
Who deploys the Bushytails?
        (Who's put two million bucks in jail?)
O foolish fox to impound The Cat.

The moon is down, night blacks the sky.
        The rabbits parley, and the foxes try
from their high-maintenance ebony halls
        to flush the rabbits out in fall.
They heat their pots and their olive oil,
        compute the time for a rabbit to boil,
and send out arsonist vipers to burn
        whatever's left, so there's nothing to mourn.
But up ahead there stands The Cat.

War after war, death piled on death,
        salt on the field kills the fox's earth;
bitter wind and brutal snow
        tear the valley to pieces. 'No,
not us!' cry the birds as they vanish south
        uncounted, taking a bird's way out.
ALL POWER TO THE FOX COLLECTIVE! —
        force corrupts mind! 'The Immaculate Death
of The Cat'--lies from a fox's mouth.

Out of the dark comes a gentle voice
        singing a freedom song. 'Gladys,'
he sings, 'while small-souled politicians
        bully the world into war and confusion,
no one of conscience can avoid a call
        that promises equality and peace.'
Half-forgotten like the tune itself,
        his ghost flares up as dawn comes on
and The Cat leads the dance on the public lawn.

The Bar & the Mirror at the Folies Bergères

Unbridled pleasure seems undemocratic
especially if it's stamped with royal cachet.
Some say the long-lost past was aristocratic
    (time, too, has its fashions of the day).

Does history contradict itself? Well then, it does.
Rose-petalled faces smile in pantomime
like lovers shaking with each other's news.
    Deaf women run about like ordinary fools.

The pure-in-heart applaud from Paradise.
And the hyper-rich behind their opera glasses
watch the night tremble over the pit, then rise
    with the moon above the naked masses

writhing under the chandelier
like drunken carp in a pond.
The barmaid is lapis lazuli;
    her eyes, two wet, black stones.

O dark excesses! Unnatural love!
Cold weather's necessities!
St. Anselm's silly proof!
    Frock-coated dolphins mock the sea.

Ladies, take off your pearly dresses!
Here comes the serpent again.
The forbidden tree is heavy
    with fruit and surrounded by hungry men.

Beware the dog beneath the skin.
At the end nature takes out
even the language it put in.
    Black holes are hot and shut.

I, too, wear black, mourning my life.
The moon circles my eyes.
All-night artists orbit in grooves,
   then flame out like meteorites.

The Blue Cat Takes Over From Miss Lonelyhearts

There's always absolutely nobody.
Nothing never shifts for less nor mo:
You can swing as high as you want in the apple tree--
hi heigh-ho high and gee low--
      but the spring of a thing is eternally so,
      perfectly yes and perfectly no.

Your half-sized face in the mirror thinks you a phantom
projection, more fiction than fact. Your self behind glass
cooquericoos cuckoos. While Cuckold, Boast of the Bantams,
      hails Hollywood passions
      and Hekate hydrogen-bombs a new class,
      you pull your pants over your impossible ass.

Love explodes in hot elastic weather.
Can you count your toes in black fluorescent light?
A draw will quit a magnet; a wing load leave its feathers;
      politicians soon forget old victory sites:
      at dawn the sun hauls gravity tight
      to the top, drops it down every night.

The Birdwatcher

There must be order among chickadees
lest the reality of melting snow
be irresistible, their calls
        the illusion of nightingales.

What exotic costumes on plain birds,
sumptuous occasions of nonsense,
parade of inversions, *et cetera*.
        Nuthatches leak upside-down.

Who festooned the trees with fireworks?
Hang sparklers or camellias.
Let's sleep in each other's arms
        as a fleet of peacocks comes sailing
        across the green digital sea.

May Day in Moscow

The Blue Cat Conducts Some Political Archaeology

'I lay,' he says. 'I lie,' he corrects. 'The past
has disappeared in the Alexander Garden.
Oh, scarlet tulips guard tall Finnish firs
and sentinels in greatcoats guard old Lenin,

but in fact the Revolution has unwound
in lies and lilacs. Nightingales sing in the oaks
as if fairy tales turned into real-life stories
and Sleeping Beauty reached up from the book

to draw the frog face to her, lips to lips,
as newlyweds beside the Unknown Soldier
kneel to a past that never can be known.
The deputies who pass the Spassky Tower
make up a company of professional lovers
        acting out the betrayals of each one.'

The Blue Cat Calls a Contry Dance

'I danced every figure until the morning pried up the sun with a crowbar.'
--Jeremiah Story

I
The Garden of Babylon

Places all, kits, cats, and toms
bow and curtsey, manners on
allemande left, a dos-si-dos
swing your partner, round you go
        pick 'em up and put 'em down
        stop when you get back to town.

        lady right, clockwise round
        gent goes left, counter bound
        down to the Green Zone, skip on through
        pass the killers as they pass you
        grab the gas can standing there
        pick the kind man on the square
        you swing him and he swings you
        make a circle two by two
        Persians on the ends dive up and under
        star in the middle, star of wonder
        Yankees shoot, not knowing what to do
        every survivor shakes a shoe
                allemande left with corners all
                grand right and left around the hall
                bring back the art, home to Baghdad
                heart still heavy, feet getting glad
                everybody swing.

        second round, same old thing
        pretty little feet and a 'copter's wing
        one for the money, one for the show
        two go where the greenbacks grow
        gent swings lady, lady swings gent

poor man pays the rich man's rent
you swing me and I swing you
pumping oil is good for you
Persians on the ends dive up and under
star in the middle, star of wonder
Yankees shoot, not knowing what to do
every survivor shakes a shoe
        allemande left with corners all
        grand right and left around the hall
        bring back the art, home to Baghdad
        heart still heavy, feet getting glad
        everybody swing.

third couple circle where the bombs land
hand-to-hand balance on the sand
'can't ever get enough of you'
'who's who' and 'who knows you'
gas can gone, cook oil too
electricity cut, water tank dry
checkpoint death has a trigger eye
waiting for me, waiting for you
Persians on the ends dive up and under
star in the middle, star of wonder
Yankees shoot, not knowing what to do
every survivor shakes a shoe
        allemande left with corners all
        grand right and left around the hall
        bring back the art, home to Baghdad
        heart still heavy, feet getting glad
        everybody swing.

thousands dead, we're coming round the bend
down by the river where the warpath ends
history a-making, where's a better view
bodies in armour, torture-minded screws
men for the killing, children left to grieve
you're now Adam, you play Eve
doomsday's coming, the book said so
but if you ask me I don't know
Persians on the ends dive up and under

    star in the middle, star of wonder
    Yankees shoot, not knowing what to do
    every survivor shakes a shoe
          allemande left with corners all
          grand right and left around the hall
          bring back the art, home to Baghdad
          heart still heavy, feet getting glad
          dance the night through, then when you're done
          away you go, too—that's number one.

II
Pop Goes the Weasel

Round and round
the village green
the soldiers march
          in line
as on a clock
the fancy hands
in quantum leaps
          keep time
a bomb goes off
two girls go wild
thirteen more
          quadrille
when suddenly
by the teacher's bench
POP! goes the
          overkill

    Round and round
    the stubborn sun
    the rocky planets
             gyrate
    and all the moons
    that are pure gas
    spin off to start to
             migrate
    here in the dark
    the universe

          is playing blind
                         man's rout
          when suddenly
          by the speaker's bench
          POP! the moon's
                         knocked out

Round and round
the Milky Way
nervy nebulae
                careen
dragging their tails
in silver pails
lined with trinitroto-
                luene
which fills the sky
with fabulous pies
of red-hot shrapnel
                sprouts
that in one burst
do their worst
of rubbing thousands
                out

          Round and round
          two atoms go
          in intergalactic
                         space
          like a mini-man
          and a mini-woman
          wearing a mini
                         face
          but down the line
          by first design
          from bottom to the
                         top
          there'll soon go round
          the giant sound
          of the universal
                         pop!

Now everybody swing
                                     if it's the last thing you do--
'that's the way the money goes'--
                            then you stop, too.

The Cat Remembers One of His Heroes

The moon is failing, the leaves are falling
    in their October round,
and we have sailed to the island of grief and sorrow
    on barren ground
where the young die before the old
    and rivers run upside down.

    Dead, dead, his grace is dead;
    from his face, the fineness fled;
    the body stiffed, untalented;
    the heart a stone lashed to his head.

He lies in state in the frozen light
    of the past like a long-legged lord
laid out for a nap on a stone sarcophagus;
    his name spins toward
extinction, and roses and rice from old lovers
    turn to dust on the floor.

    Dead, dead, his grace is dead;
    from his face, the fineness fled;
    the body stiffed, untalented;
    the heart a stone weighing down the bed.

He dressed his piano with photographs
    like a ship with signal flags,
trimmed his face to fit a golden mask
    like bronze-greaved Achilles, who plucked
a lyre in Elysium while he in his living room
    jazzed 'The Maple Leaf Rag.'

    Dead, dead, his grace is dead;
    from his face, the fineness fled;
    the body stiffed, untalented;
    the heart purged, the backside bled.

Turned and returned night after night
        to the dark by soft brown hands
pliant with pain and impertinent to death,
        three times he watched the Great Wain
circle the north, then deposit his soul
        in the sea in a warm dawn.

        Dead, dead, his grace is dead;
        from his face, the fineness fled;
        the body stiffed, untalented;
        the heart an unfathomable lead.

Like the sashes that hold a king together,
        or the rivers binding the wet earth,
the wind was his girdle and his lifting weather;
        let the wind now shake out dust-mop death.
At the foot of his bed each night the old dog
        lays her head on her paws.

        Dead, dead, his grace is dead;
        from his face, the fineness fled;
        the body stiffed, untalented;
        the heart some artificial red.

The great body quickly cooled;
        the smile that once upon a time
each day and night had lured a lover
        into eternity fell with the face;
not even the fast talk of a Fool
        could fill the wasted space.

        Dead, dead, his grace is dead;
        from his face, the fineness fled;
        the body stiffed, untalented;
        the heart a stone, a stone at his head.

Chained like a dog to yesterday's news,
        he flew across an imaginary stage
behind the living, his life reduced
        to picturing his lost days.
As the sun set, the contrails turned blood orange,
        then smoke grey, then vanished in dark blue.

Fortune-telling

As the full moon rises, the national twilight
    floats down river. Old Glory sinks
behind the city's gold-skin towers.
    Imagine Puss-in-Boots dying
        in the spider web of his father's blindness,
        cat going for cat.

So kindred slaughter each other mindlessly;
    blood flows, religion leeches each house;
hatred mutilates high-mindedness;
    the green hills of New England
        and the fish-filled southern ocean
        go dry like the moon.

Out of the ruins, from the far side of West Mountain
    I see words rise as bent as a rainbow,
bearing a strawberry heart with two green eyes
    to induce, by fancy, our vision of peace,
        in which life's virtually satisfied
        and reality has a ninety-nine year lease.

The Cat Ponders Joining a Picket Line

This work was mine
it came by chance
      like a bead of red glass
           rolled high on a beach
      by an angry sea
      like a bird nest passed
from hand to hand—
           homemade things

I would if I could have
come signing life
      like a warm wind
      like unfurling waves
      where a long-legged ruff
      dancing on spindrift
                clocks the sand—
      O arbiter

Our labour our hands
      our names lost
      in heavy noise
      in the line assembling
      the ocean's roll
           around the clock
      the misplaced facts—
           the waste of time

The Blue Cat Blues

The river rose, done took my house,
the Devil made off with my jack;
sail or swim like a fish—
how'll I ever get it back?

Chorus:
>No way today
>to wash the blackness from the sea;
>no way, no way
>to take the blueness out of me.

The levee's broke, no more canal,
the Gulf has swallowed up town hall;
no place safe, no dry land—
Satan's won the Power Ball.

Chorus:
>No way today
>to wash the blackness from the sea;
>no way, no way
>to take the blueness out of me.

My girl run off where livin's free,
FEMA got the best of me;
whites drove out, blacks swam in—
gone, long gone racial harmony.

Chorus:
>No way today
>to wash the blackness from the sea;
>no way, no way
>to take the blueness out of me.

Lower Ninth was drowned, our town,
lost my parrot and my pup;
jack all gone, no help coming—
no one here to build the levees up.

Chorus:
>No way today
>to wash the blackness from the sea;
>no way, no way
>to take the blueness out of me.

An Invisible Man Addresses the Cat

Brown is invisible.
Neither to see nor be seen—
minarets like shadow
monsters on the walls,
the sun cruel for burning
a hole in the middle of the day,
a black hole
of doubt and darkness,
the camels lost,
the soldiers run away.

The sun sinks at the end of each day,
then like a great fish rises
out of the desert in the red morning.
'Welcome, Sun!' a man shouts to the noise
though to him it's no more than a warning
of darker darkness to come.

(In physics it's true that what can't be seen must exist,
but who has worked out the equations for history?)
In his mind he still hears Umm Kulthum chanting the Qur'an;
in the oil fields, the children are deaf and dumb.

Does he know what it's like to cut out an eye with a bomb?
Can he feel what it's like to gouge out an eye with a thumb?
Ignorance and violence strut together,
cakewalk partners from classical drama
and other horror shows in which the blood
of actors substitutes for martyrs
and the good die young.
This is his first death.
Surely the others will be like it,
but how can he know whose report to believe,
how many there'll be, for how long?

He hears smells, tastes words, touches sounds.
He feels the air change colour.
Some say they'll yet save his sight;
some, they can't.
If tomorrow in righteous anger
he rips the world apart like paper,
there's small surprise,
but for the time being he has few regrets,
no sense of having lost
(though losing what is death to hide),
only a longing to do such good
that no one can forget.

Hear what the Lord said:
Revenge is up to me; I'll pay back well.
Fair enough: no man
can decide how much is due.
The worst isn't what has been done
but what others don't yet know they'll do.

He wonders what he looks like:
Am I also the blind boy in *al-Ayyam*
in tattered shirt coming down the street?
Will I dictate to the world the contents of my mind?
On this street there's no looking glass—
I can't see out, you can't see in—
there's no one stepping through.
Indeed, because I'm brown you don't see me,
and because I'm going blind I can't see you.

The Auctioneer

Evening, ladies; evening, gents;
        salute you by the dozen, embrace you by the score;
we've got things here worth fifteen cents
        and others worth a million more.
Get your numbers, don't miss a chance
        to bear the rifle Captain Brown once bore
        or touch the lace that trimmed Miss Marilyn's underpants.
When playing cards were bare on back
        folks filled 'em in as invites to the local square;
now here's a photo that will pack
        your venue with a hundred cats who'll dare
play the G-string on this human cello—
this ain't the F-clef on a bowl of jello—
        Who'll give me ten? Ten! Make it twenty.
Sixty. Eighty. A hundred! No *argumenty*
        from me against this turbaned queen of the night!
        Going once; going twice; sold to her lover on my right!

Draw close now, picture a real-life story
        about the deal of your dreams that still hangs verily
ghost-like every day in squamous glory,
        then sit at this early American secretary
where Great-great-grandfather Cat on his feline ass
        signed the law that stopped rebellion in western Mass.
He who sits at this desk pilots the nation
        on the wings of change using the rudder of chance,
so be to your friends a friendly inspiration
        and make dens of lions out of hills of ants.
For you patriots who hold your history dear
        a thousand's nothing for ten pigeon holes—
yes, ma'am, a thousand—twelve fifty—now fifteen clear—
        two thousand—two—your friends'll say you stole it—
going once, going twice, as Dolly Madison wrote,
        to a lady to use in getting out the vote.

An auction like this you truly have to see—
    the Pembroke shaped top, the period cherry chests,
the drop leaf Queen Anne, the inlaid mahogany
    demilune with leaves, the glass, the finest
Persians and the rarest Chinese silk—
    all brought together by a dealer's taste.
Here, friends, before you is a man's life's work
    offered at the values of today.
Terms: cash or credit card, like everywhere
    you shop and save. A genuine antique beauty
gives your simple, modern parlour a noble air.
    One girandole is every husband's duty.
Man comes and goes; his furniture remains;
    we buy and sell the shadows of the past;
how inspiring the tracks of our toy trains,
    and how we're grateful for lovely things at last.

The Cat Advances to a Higher Degree

On dit is how the French begin
        when they want to skip original sin;
the Russians use impersonal verbs
        as bland as homeopathic herbs;
in Rome one does as Romans do;
        with Rats one screws or gets screwed.

These days in the Reign of Rats
        all failures fall on raghead cats;
the only way to duck the blame
        is to become a famous name.
Did Rats swear alien aviation
        brought down the pillars of the nation,

then send Cats forth from The Polyhedron
        for 'Peace,' 'Security,' and 'Freedom'
though kittens starved and thousands died
        and half the great Euphrates dried?
To counteract the primal liars
        the Blue Cat set out to climb higher.

The stars above the Wealthy Dominion
        like horoscopes shape public opinion,
and each acolyte in the Church of Power
        aspires to be the Cat of the Hour,
but justice and equality
        have become commodities,

so a Cat with a sheepskin Ph D
        can buy and sell celebrities.
No animal on earth's so wise
        as the great Blue Cat with great blue eyes
in whose workshop on the wall
        hangs a diploma mailed out last fall.

He submitted a form and a money order
    to a faith-based college near the border,
ten days later got a scroll to keep,
    and tiger-eyed the CEO of the heap—
purveyor of catnip, pilot-in-chief,
    keeper of mousetraps, pope of belief—

thought to himself: *if we don't lead we'll be led;*
    if we trust in one 'great' leader we're lost.
So he cried, 'Rebels all, alive or dead!
    Empower the young, let them become boss.
Abandon all parties not morally true,
    and vote yourselves in in Permanent Blue.'

The Heavenly Kingdom

The Cat that one day was born from the sky
        sailed all the oceans East and West
at the tip of a topmast where he flew as gulls fly
        and proved to the cynics his nautical zest,
    singing:
            yo ho ho the wind blows free,
            o for a life on the rolling sea.

In later years he lay still and looked,
        his paws tucked in on a window ledge,
till sadly he found that he'd been booked
        into Life Beyond on the Heavenly Edge,
    singing:
            wherever I was the wind blew free
            for porpoise and me on the rolling sea.

Heaven was dry he soon found out;
        no matter how often it thundered and rained
not a drop for old sailors was ever poured out
        and not a fig was given for life on the main,
    singing:
            up here in Heaven the wind blows free
            to save poor sailors from that old devil sea.

No one cared whether or not he opined;
        wherever he shopped he was sternly told,
'You're nobody special, go stand in line
        like dogs in their kennel and sheep in their fold,'
    singing:
            cats go down when the wind blows free
            'cause cats can't handle the rolling sea.

His pension too small to keep him in fish,
        his taxes too high for him to afford
a Levittown box, a car, or a dish,
        he lived by a bridge beneath an old board,
    singing:

remember the days when the wind blew free?
o bring back my oceans, bring an ocean to me.

Eve came over with Adam, that bristly tom,
    forgotten and grey and bent from despair;
they bitched about the Lord's grievous wrongs
    and Job-like swore they had nothing to wear,
singing:
    if ever the wind were true and free,
    mankind would be sailing the rolling sea.

'Arise and be counted!' they cried to the drinkers
    who were quaffing the suds at the local brew-pub,
'Rabelais laid out an abbey of thinkers
    and Marx proposed putting workers on top,'
singing:
    revolution's the wind that blows a cat free
    to the New World across the rolling sea.

The boys in the back looked up from their cards
    as the freshly interred look up from their graves;
one soul raised the ante but promptly was called,
    and one angel declared, 'Sweet Jesus saves,'
singing:
    this is the life where the wind blows free
    in the heavenly roll on the rolling sea.

'O fools,' they replied, 'you know not what you do,
    wasting your days indoors in the dark;
Earth's as repressive as Heaven, that's true,
    but at least when it rains there's Noah's Ark,'
singing:
    yo ho ho the wind blows free,
    o for a life on the rolling sea.

The Cat Leads a Revival Meeting

Over on Ninth there's a half-hidden bar
between Phoebe, clairvoyant, and Block, H. R.;
every night from city-wide desert places
philosophical types crowd The Oasis;
'drink deep or taste not,' forewarned A. Pope,
so they come for martinis with packets of dope
        and try to drain The Oasis.

One evening in walks this giant Cat,
a hook in his belt, a plume in his hat,
a chip on one shoulder, a tomahawk on the other—
a swaggering, louche, and ruffian mother
with twirlable whiskers and a tail a yard long
and a baritone voice that burst into song
        for justice for all brothers.

'You here for our regular Saturday jam?'
the boys asked, 'or the open-mike monthly slam?'
The Cyrano Cat bowed low with panache:
'I dispute all your titles; I come here to bash
in the heads of state and the feet that follow
and prove to you cause-and-effect is hollow,
        so much intellectual trash.'

'You and who else?' cried Ralph from the rear
as Timmy and Tom put the piano in gear,
starting up a duet of 'Who Owns the Streets'
like the words affirmed some real-estate feat,
which soon the whole crowd was singing and humming
while staunch in the centre the Cat began drumming
        and thumping his seven-league feet.

'Enough of this nonsense!' Morgan exclaimed
(an uptown professor with a national name),
'if you've come to dispute, let us prove who is who;
so, beware of what will happen to you
when your logic falters, your arguments fail,
but instead of salting you off in some jail
        we wipe the floor with you.'

The Cat bent a knee as he unhooked his axe,
replying with vigour to verbal attacks
and telling the teacher whatever he tries
when his heart's on fire, smoke gets in his eyes;
'indeed,' said the Cat as he set himself down,
'language as falsehood has captured the town,
        your truth is nothing but lies.'

'Begin,' said the doc; 'if you've something to say
it'll have to come out in the usual way,
because nothing exists that cannot be said,
as the living are living because they're not dead;
and the proof of a pudding is not in consumption
but the patterned coherence of the cook's gumption
        and the chocolate spots on his head.'

'Here's a song,' said The Cat unfurling his tongue,
'that only the deaf have ever heard sung:
No matter what you have on your plate
you'll soon be off to the Pearly Gates
where Zeus hands out free golden wings
        and bottled water from the Pierian Spring,
        and phylogeny is fate.

'So what you must do,' said the Cat with a swirl
and a swish of the fuzzy bernous of his tail,
'is give praise to God—be He ever exalted—
for making sure every dickie bird's salted
and the fish in the lake under His care
being infidels won't remember where
        the Prince of Peace once faltered.'

'O love!' cried the Cat as he rolled on the ground,
'again the Spirit is working me round.
I burn inside!' he shrieked to the crowd,
'as if the Lord God—praise Him all we're allowed—
were lighting my soul for Paradise.
Open your ears; open your eyes;
        off with weeds and shrouds!'

He pulled on a kefayeh and an Anglican cope
and turned to read what the moving hand wrote:
'Mene mene tekel upharsin—
Belshazar was cooked by holy arson;
greed destroyed him, my skeptical friends,
but charity hath life giving ends—
        all blessings from Heaven's parson.'

He lay there exhausted watching out of one eye
what the boys would make of it. By and by
they shuffled and coughed and said, 'You know,
you can't trust a cat but you can sure like his show.'
They passed the hat and bought him a glass
of lager, which left him a white moustache.
        He bowed and turned to go.

'O Cat,' they said, 'we'd believe what we heard
if we knew that the world would end in a Word.'
The Cat waved good-by and gave a big grin:
'How will it end? How did it begin?'
He stiffened his tail and spun out the door
and hasn't been seen on Ninth anymore.
        And the boys went back to their gin.

The Blue Cat Hits the Ballot Box

The Cat went into the high-school gym
    to vote for a ticket politically blue;
they gave him a sheet of white paper and said,
    "You'll need a plain yellow pencil, too."

    'Ain't I been here before?' thought the Cat by the door;
        'if it's like last time, forget it;
    whoever has hopes for real change must still
        keep on fighting to get it.'

He picked up a pencil and made forty black marks
    and surveyed the white ballot when he got through;
'x' in the boxes—boxes of 'x'es
    were forty square dreams half black and half blue.

    'Back in my youth,' thought the Cat in the booth,
        'it was always like last time; forget it;
    whoever has wanted real change has had
        to keep fighting to get it.'

He laid down the pencil and pulled back the curtain
    and folded the ballot (as instructed) in two,
and wondered if ever the good cat he dreamed of
    would turn out to be half black and half blue.

    'Sure, I've been there before,' thought the Cat out the door,
        'I'll never forget it;
    all my lives I've been hoping for change and I still
        will keep fighting to get it.'

A Blue Study: Fiscal Policy vs. Monetary

At first it cost a nickel,
        then went up to a dime;
before you knew it took two bits
        to dial a local line:

> *life's been getting dearer*
> *by anti-revolutionary bounds—*
> *the rich are rising up*
> *and the poor are falling down.*

Inflation shrank our savings,
        then the subprime scandal burst,
the feds bailed out their banker friends
        and left us in the dirt:

> *life's been getting dearer*
> *by anti-revolutionary bounds—*
> *the rich are rising up*
> *and the poor are falling down.*

Gas is now two-fifty,
        half the price of bread—
I wish I had my nickels back
        or my old house instead:

> *life's been getting dearer*
> *by anti-revolutionary bounds—*
> *the rich are rising up*
> *and the poor are falling down.*

Acknowledgements

The Blue Cat Walks the Earth was first published by Azul Editions in 2007. Grateful acknowledgement is also made to the editors of the following journals and anthologies in which these poems originally appeared:

American Poetry Journal, American Poetry Review, caesura, Carquinez Poetry Review, Chrysalis, For New Orleans, Free Lunch, Margie, Marlboro Review, Michigan Quarterly Review, Modern Poetry Review, Modern Poetry Studies, New Criterion, Panoply, Poets Against War, Poetry: A Magazine of Verse, Seeds of Fire, September 11th, The Sewanee Review, Vallum: a Journal of Contemporary Poetry, We Begin Here: Poems for Palestine and Lebanon.